Structure and Trade

Another boom ahead
CV Deepamadhvi

Oil

- Demand is weak in West and strong in middle East
- Iranian nuclear deal is not letting the best risk management
- Prices are very uphill with sanctions

Economic cruise missile

- European and Asian research efforts will knock down the future gaps in the growth opportunities for the advanced and emerging markets leaving the third world countries with the onus to be fast accomodating mass consumer market

Policies are short term

- What is going to be in the world after 3, 6 or 12 months?
- Not policies for they shall change
- Customer knowledge and expectations of the market stay at driving the patterns in the fast changing global economy.

High inflation

- Consumption is the best victim and worst beneficiary
- Foreign investors and regulations transition from commission to fee based model
- Volume has been more in USA and Asia for investment flows thus keeping the global inflation upward

Consumption is fragile

- Most people don't complete the consumption of products and services, either they switch midway, change preferences or call it off
- Such expenses are having great research and experimental advantages.
- Currencies will take a new debilitating effect on the best systematic used currentcy.

Potential of market

- Assess savings and spend patterns and needs against potential of individuals and businesses
- Evaluation of products and offer to understand new market evolution
- Utilisation of skills and unemployment rate will be able to guide for productivity scope

Dividend changes

- The retained earnings and deductions for taxes decide the company contribution and change in government support besides increase or decrease in the revenue and profits give precise information on market capitalisation and share price after expenses for dividend distribution.

Sensible manager

- You are not sensible to manage but be sure to be checked and managed by customers because a customer has unorganised raw data that makes sense more than a whole organised database of the company.

After a single year

- Transparent trade policy and procedures will take domestic and international industry in the shelter of strictly strong strategic structures of infrastructure fulfillment, employment expansion overseas and easy transition to annual economic growth check posts.

Inclusive of stock markets

- The best way to get the latest flash of stock markets is not available spreads for trading but the other factors like limits, volume and weight of each category (of equity, commodities) to calculate the total combined effect of activities on the economic growth.

Risk exposure

- Markets are able to cover risks and provide easy benefits to companies better than ever so firms are exposing themselves to get hedging, forecast, volatility, global trade and development benefits

Temper of interest rates

- The inherent nature of yields and price volatility drives the rise and fall of interest to affect the microeconomics and macroeconomics of industrial trade structures in the direction of integrating nations to global relevance and consumer interest must be protected in the furtherance of economic interests.

Reactions of yields

- Longer term borrowing will increase by the low yield curves
- Market waves will turn on the side of liquidity and consumer spending that is the best way to bigger margins
- Rising prices will find yields on low.

Local movement

- Citizens and foreigners both try to give the best to their country
- Transparent trade policy and easy terms can do wonders to international economic interests furtherance to get the latest technologies to preserve local strength.

Future change is not far

- Yields and price volatility would be moving in multiple correlation in a short period of time
- Gains will go into economic growth, losses will send corrective signals
- The intelligence of economy will be built by intellectual machine and freer manager thinking for economic development.

USA vs middle East

- Oil and dollar fights for the dominance in global economy relevance could be soon replaced by the technology vs human dignity in direct influence of information behind market movements leaving the rest of the factors as placeholders merely.

Exchange traded funds

- Mutual funds and bond funds can be found profitable trading welldiversified and yield oriented
- Margin and risk return on investment innovation will take a new turn to get better opportunity for future.

Fund ecosystem

- Never allow deficiency of resources to be a case for structural failures
- Feed the value chains and participants in the entire ecosystem to get trade services with affordable policy and procedural change
- Assign resources and act upon response of every change factor.

Next panes

- Some lists are added with factors that are managing the current century transition from global to glocal economy (every country is small global economy)

A-list

- Automation
- Agility
- Acceptance

- B-list
- Buyer
- Business
- Bug

C-list

- Currencies
- Change
- Crisis

- D-list
-   Distribution
-   Dynamics
-   Decision

E-list

- Experience
- Expectations
- Economy

- F-list
-   Feed of data
-   Forex
-   Family of business and customer

Glist

- Geography
- Geo navigation system
- Goods and services

- Hlist
- Hi-tech
- Human resources
- Health care

I-list

- Innovation
- International trade
- Investment

- Jlist
- Jargon
- Joint venture
- Jit

Klist

- Knowledge
- Kaizen
- Key policy

- L-list
- Localisation
- Liberalisation
- Library of documentation

M-list

- Marketpower
- Monetary policy
- Mapping

- N-list
- Nation
- Need
- Neutrality of trade

O-LIST

- Organisational structure
- Output
- Opportunity

- P-list
-   Product
-   Process
-   Provider, policy, price

Q list

- Quick view of trade policy
- Questions
- Quality

- R list
-   Resources
-   Rectification of the errors
-   Rating

S list

- Stipulation
- Structure
- Stock

- T list
-    Transparent
-    Time-bound
-     Trade

U list

- Ultra-high tech trade
- Usage guidelines
- Unitary structures

- V list
-   Value
-   Volatility
-    Verity

W list

- Workshop
- Wish
- Window project (quick project on trade venture)

- X list
- Xcess (apt taxes)
- Xtra strategy
- Xpertise

Y list

- Yields curve
- Year-on-year results
- Yardsticks

- Z list
-   Zero stock/defects
-   Zeal
-   Zen

Success factors

- Trade policy in favour of fair play that encourages exchange of information, technology, goods and services with nations.
- Volume and demand-supply should balance out losses of the cross-border transactions without conditions on economy.

Practices

- Trade must be derived and protected, not policy driven but national interest driven structures can grow industry in real multi country global relevance and consumer interest in our standardization of the best product and service exchange or redistribution of resources.

Tools

- Interest and yield revaluation to daily trade imbalance calculation for your future plans
- Product and customer satisfaction guarantee from customer demanded criteria
- Cross-country analysis of variance in the commerce and industry trends.

Co trade

- Competition aims to respond with mutual interest in combining the effects and efforts on research, trade and investment in the local and international markets as the beginning of competition in co- takes origin in 'together' and the same applies to company that has to work for domestic followed by global growth.

Full track trade

- Allow to trade and develop the best skills and knowledge for the global improvement in the productivity and quality of goods and services, not to let superficial growth of commerce and industry in consumer connection alone.

Trade measure

- Not light and heavy but the quality of exchanges and returns to welcome the opportunity with rapport and trust of mutual interest in combining cross national association for global cultural heritage formation of a different kind to encourage the growth of your and surrounding economies.

Policy drivers

- Growth in the collaborating countries to manage the intertrade conditions should balance out the loopholes of micro and macro environmental policy driven by government and market uncertainty of enabling trade in merely to get through the needs and deficiency of the nations.

- Consumer preferences and industry cycles drive trade policy in favour of fair structure.

Structure sums

- The organisational issues with your company can be solved by your infrastructure expansion and technology growth in the future so on the same language that combination of these with commerce possibilities, cross border cultural adaptation or multination priority to exchange skills, knowledge, goods in excess can solve the problems in structural failures of trade.

Cross border cultural adaptation

- Product includes the best usage guidelines but it gives better opportunity for seller to arrange for customisation based on cultural differences between the two trading nations after leaving the original manufacturer specifications for the brand differentiation in favour of restoring national uniqueness.

Trade gears

- Cross border cultural differences should be respected
- Cross national regulations should be friendly
- Customer service in exchange because both sides are each other's customer and not a buyer and seller alone, should be addressed in balancing the budget limitations and needs of your own nation with those of the other countries.

Unutilized resources

- Nations can exchange the unused inputs and outputs of utilising them to 9et the best cross cultural impact of adaptation and mitigation measures to protect against potential losses of the extra cost to not exploiting the best of your own resources.

Trade genesis

- The government of the willing nations should be one to commence the initiative in favour of fair play structure and strategy to enhance the dealings with products at the next step to further business by disinvestment options and starting MNC.

Trade allows strategy

- Countries with the new influence on cultural and social mechanisms of globalisation can inspire international trade and investment by comparing, competing, utilising, collaborating on the global research, resources and information technology for multidimensional synergistic trade.

Trade has a structure

- Bring your own nation and its richness of the most important thing in product or service in providing specific guidance and receiving support from the best of other countries to manage the global market uncertainty with the limitless information and possibilities. The best benefits of global trade come to the nations in adopting a structure of the international trade compliance and relevance.

Trade is not business

- International trade and investment is not business and customer thing but essentially exchange of information, money and product to the one lacking, needing, inviting or promoting the best resources, talent and skills to work with expertise in developing the potential for growth in other countries.

Trade assurance

- Of trust and respect
- Of confidence and self-esteem
- Of control and management
- Of automation and prevention of resources wastage

Trade is joint policy

- It's not another monetary policy and procedural change but the quality dealings with other countries via exchange of information and technology or goods and services.

Noun trade

- The new trade policy driven by exchange of branded products that are not different or dissimilar in many ways, is gaining importance in the next step to cross cultural trade where the best preference goes to noun based products against famous names, places or things.

Deal to international trade

- The inherent compliance and regulatory affairs tend to remain part of international trade and countries with deal tactics compare best to generate higher exchange of goods.

Trade allows training

- Training to become an expert agent and trader can do wonders to international economic situation to best of your own nation with the proper resource utilisation and benefit distribution.

Policy drives

- Trade in merely to seek direction and law enforcement but the policy cheats for your time with the new influence on complications in the future so much to customise the deal as a favour of restoring international economic dependence.

Structure knocks

- On the international economic growth because strategy takes a backseat
- Out losses of the product and resources drawbacks of earning a new experience for free trade and investment opportunities.

Strategy talks

- Of control and management plans for next growth ventures
- About the products but not without competitive bent and advantages
- By taking trade and development to the next step in excellence.

Transparent trade aspirant

- Catch the best trade practices and worst trade preference for maximizing the accountability and returns of international trade because you can increase efficiency of you succeed in the trade preference rated as bottom rung.

More than business

- Trade is not exchanges of goods or products that your country doesn't want but of skills, Heritage, knowledge, technology, research, market drivers, purchasing power, process improvement, channel logistics and value change.

Tradenomics

- Company should remember not to waste resources and supply along recyclable resources to right globalisation open for Innovation in accepting through each nation's economic development needs.

Foreigners as sellers

- Interaction between countries can grow rough foreigners domination in MNC route of proving worth of global sellers when you see your citizens working with other nations on growth of both sides.

- See that the economic development through trade happens by allowing combination of Technological or community or cultural differences between national output of great resource strategies for user appreciation on both sides.

Make a cap

- Opt for new benchmarks and standards of products that help with the progress of other companies in the process of business changes brought for international trade participation.

ETF alternatives

- Gold with cross border arbitrage opportunity
- Other than that new business funds will be traded for oil, carbon, uranium, platinum, iron, silver, etc.
- New emotional trading fund in emotional currency

Brewing volatility

- International border laws should be flexible and balanced to get new solution for betterment against volatile conditions of competition to do cross culture trade with your business products or services.

Job opportunity

- Is for trade participants of ensuring the flow is approved, smooth and uninterrupted without disturbing trends into modern fusion of decision culture with output quality finding its way out on competition opportunity with different nations.

Buying opportunity

- The most favoured nation status could give good opportunities to buyers on terms, offers, product features or other discounts in nation treating import as opportunities hidden by challenges of expenses and price.

Hedging vs treasury

- NPA is no different than creating risk of default loss to risk zone in the process of hedging for trading maintaining a common security in treasury operations at excellence in cash management and technology alignment.

Go back from start of competition to be versatile company.

Future will find

- Increase in supply
- Tax is good
- Curve implications
- On the dollar getting strangled
- Stimulus for overseas investors due to currency hedging

- Yield ready markets are more likely to convert the threats to decisions on your portfolio management and business technology vision for future leadership in the world of financial freedom of information loopholes to get the best returns for the changing risk preferences.

Market decision

- First development that aims at international trade is no longer need or capabilities but market decision on generating unique value or company weaknesses by throwing challenges in changing your customer preferences.

Front end observations

- The company knows how much to get exploitative of new technologies or opportunities but some extra exploration as front end observation is not overemphasizing the customer role in the process of international trade.

Time horizon

- Trade terms and business changes should be balanced with time not without incremental risk management strategy for smart solutions building a common contextual integration with market trust.

Anomalies

- Exporter dumps the waste in the name of trade favouritism
- Importers smuggle and break laws of water and air for bringing cheaper stuff to sell at higher gains
- Goods will be expired in long process delay

Risk incentive

- Credit risk is worth the wait
- Portfolio diversification gives a good time to watch
- Higher rating derisks underperforming pieces
- Don't forget the case to case basis inspection
- Seek insurance and not cash.

Portfolio directions

- Combine goods in primary and secondary sectors
- Promote online trade of services in exchange of competitive knowledge and technology alignment in nations.

CapEx cycles

- Let Customer enhance competitive advantage of nations on exchanging capitals as your quick expenditures and investment gains over global trade transformation practices at the highest quality products and technologies that are talking business. Keep the cycles as short as possible.

Block the auction

- To support yields on the same upward and onward directions
- Unsecured bonds yield high of 8-10% under disruptive business model
- Secondary market takes positive feedback from primary market in risk neutral mode

Valuation

- Risks are getting compensated
- Investors face desperation
- Sudden change in the bond markets are supported by the currency valuation
- Emerging markets leaving for the customer satisfaction enter the oil from currencies.

Energy markets

- Future value of quality cross border trade could not buy solutions without innovation and inclusion of energy in the process of establishing new sources, forms of usage and support to replenish in natural and unnatural form.

Currency markets

- Host all sorts of risks, foul play and discrepancies
- More excitement and enthusiasm in a business comes from overcoming market ropewalk in currency fluctuations by allowing advanced trading position

Dollar

- Is indicative price for the large scale development of Customer through standard local currency fluctuations by depending upon the market improvement or upliftment of commerce portfolio decisions.

Yen

- Is proof of aligning market power, Technology Innovation and entrepreneurship hassle with the global goal getting green innovation but as agile enough helpful information for others to emulate, compete or exploit.

Euro

- Artificial sequence of dominance
- Sincere efforts of reaching better capabilities and potential on improving currency performance and managing market difference
- Futuristic currency when market will employ dollar alternatives.

Be comfortable

- Exposure
- Dollar weaknesses
- Changes in currencies

Traceable effects

- Utility of technology that could give customers good value with products may turn out to betterin one country and worse in the other
- Volume and price but not value can be compared across global trade.

No shock

- Inflation is going up
- Wages are not without pressure
- Expectations are not overshooting but structure change in economy is never going to be risk free

Cost indexes

- Input available in one country and used by another to be sold in the direction of getting customised in different countries can grow trained indexes for trade transformation to get multiplex cost structures of Customer gain by taking direct access to global trade participation.

Fiscal drags

- Deficit is due to hyperactivity in international trade
- Excess stability and business wastes could not be avoided in the past, nor can be in future trade.

Huge lags

- Trade terms and conditions can't afford to wait for new change within your company and Customer as your culture of trust by other nations but tradeoffs can not be ignored because of its forex impacts.

Remarkable move

- Look at market pricing
- Try to reduce unemployment rate
- See patterns of growth and inflation rate of the world economy
- Fed and markets are not unrelated to the next level of spread

Big strategy for bills

- Trade bill settlement process is asking for operational Innovation with exceptional Strategy for new solution for betterment of business communication and collaboration measures to protect environmental participation of global user.

Credit is long

- Increasing the market interest
- Adds to confusion with information or technologies
- Initiatives hold risk
- Current expectations are not same as that met.

Bond markets don't co-operate

- Trust factor is not available
- Investors and buyers don't know how to handle debt
- Foreign, corporate or individual representatives can't afford to wait for long-term benefits.

Big issues

- Threshold
- Psychological
- Expectations of market
- Growth economy

Labour costs ride

- Difference between nations on affecting international trade costs
- Main cost is not Technology but labour for new skills and retaining quality change to form good opportunities hidden by inability of business customisation.

Fixed income savior

- Trade in online financial instruments and tactics should be free of risk of default by advanced market customisation of government instruments and treasury instruments that balance between preferences, return or losses.

Equity role

- Low capital, return or losses
- Best efficiency of long-term strategic growth
- Better replacement of short-term interest or other business changes brought by changing trade expectations.

Metres reflect

- Metrics and business representatives
- Methods for optimum resource strategies
- Methodology for new business results
- Relationship between risk and issues on economic conditions of trade.

Commodity prices

- Rise for managing future inflation
- Pose risk and issues on government intervention
- Online e-commerce and digital trade transformation could give good price for products.

Exiting treasury positions

- When curves are flat, it's better to have the highest treasury investment reduced
- What short term curves say can guide to buying on strategic gain
- Renaissance to dollar rates hard, stronger dollar means more volatility and risk on vulnerable more

Turning points

- Higher interest rates cannot be guaranteed
- Equity based buying on the anvil
- Long term treasury position of higher treasury rates
- Low returns to asset markets in fixed income for low cross asset volatility could affect treasury rates

www.ingramcontent.com/pod-product-compliance
Lightning Source LLC
Chambersburg PA
CBHW020555220526
45463CB00006B/2310